THRI
CAS

Christopher J Tabraham BA, FSA Scot
Inspector of Ancient Monuments

Historic Buildings and Monuments
Scottish Development Department

Edinburgh
Her Majesty's Stationery Office

Threave Island and its castle

Introduction

`Legend and Life´

Legend has it that Threave Island was the home of the ancient rulers of Galloway a thousand and more years ago. Today there is no trace of their fortress. The island's natural defensive qualities were not lost on Sir Archibald Douglas when, in 1369, he was charged by his monarch, David II, with the task of bringing the hostile Gallovidians to order. That he was largely successful in this is doubtless attributable, in no small part, to the presence deep in Galloway of his castle at Threave. By his death in 1400, Archibald was unquestionably the most powerful magnate in southern Scotland, and Galloway was the real foundation of that power. When the House of Stewart took steps to overthrow the Black Douglas a half century after Archibald's death, it was at Threave that the final act in the drama unfolded. The other Douglas strongholds fell easily to King James II, but Threave withstood a two-month siege in the summer of 1455 before the garrison surrendered. The Black Douglases were finally destroyed, their estates forfeited.

The present castle ruins are testimony to this powerful aristocratic family. They are in addition highly instructive of the development of Scottish secular architecture in the later medieval and early modern period. Both the original tower house and the later artillery fortification are significant benchmarks in that development.

The tall, forbidding tower house that dominates the island, built for Archibald Douglas soon after his elevation to the lordship of Galloway in 1369, was amongst the first to be constructed in Scotland. Its compact, self-contained arrangement of the principal residential accommodation, economically achieved, was ideally suited to those troubled days and helped to establish this new fashion in baronial architecture which was to become so prevalent later. The artillery fortification, wrapped around his grandfather's tower by William Douglas almost a century after, was likewise an innovation, and a remarkably sophisticated one, combining a defensive provision for the traditional weaponry, cross-bows and long-bows, with the new-fangled and still largely experimental invention, the gun.

After the overthrow of the Black Douglases, Threave played an insignificant role in Scotland's history and, following the surrender of its garrison to the Covenanters in 1640, the castle was rendered uninhabitable and the island finally abandoned. The ruin was taken into state care shortly before World War I—one of the first great ruined castles to be protected.

Threave Castle is one of a number of castles and churches associated with the Black Douglas family which are in the care of the Secretary of State for Scotland: Bothwell Castle near Glasgow; Balvenie Castle in Grampian; Aberdour Castle in Fife; Lochleven Castle near Kinross; Hermitage Castle in Liddesdale; Lincluden Collegiate Church near Dumfries; St Bride's Church, Douglas; and Sweetheart Abbey, on the Solway Firth.

This guide-book contains a history of the castle, and a tour, which begins on page 11. Plans of the castle appear on the inside back cover.

A seal matrix, c 1403, made for Princess Margaret, daughter of Robert III and wife of Archibald, 4th earl of Douglas, found on the island. The inscription – sig Mergareta Dowglas – encircles a shield bearing the arms of the 4th earl (on the left) and the Royal Arms of Scotland (the lion rampant).

'The Island Fortress'

The castle of Black Douglas

The castle of Threave stands on a low grassy island in the River Dee some 14 km upstream from the burgh and port of Kirkcudbright. The natural strength of the island doubtless made it a place of habitation from an early time though there is as yet no evidence to indicate when this was. The very name suggests that this might have been as long ago as the sixth or seventh centuries AD for 'Threave', anciently called 'Trief', is derived from the Old Welsh 'Tref', meaning 'homestead'. Old Welsh was the native tongue of Galloway prior to the arrival of a Gaelic-speaking people during the seventh century. Tradition has it that the island was a residence for Fergus, lord of Galloway, and his descendants from the eleventh century onwards. This may have been the residence referred to by the historian John of Fordun as having been burnt by Edward de Brus, brother of Robert, after his defeat of Roland and the Gallovidians beside the River Dee in 1308.

Nevertheless it is not until the fifteenth century that the name first makes its appearance in the written record, as the place where Archibald 'the Grim', third earl of Douglas, died on Christmas Eve, 1400. It is generally stated that the present castle was built on the orders of Archibald following his elevation to the lordship of Galloway in September, 1369. Galloway, comprising the land lying between the rivers Nith in the east and Cree in the west, had been a problem to the Scottish crown for a long time. During the wars of independence, at the beginning of the fourteenth century, the Gallovidian chiefs had sided with Balliol and the English, principally because of their hatred of Robert de Brus. The rebellion was put down by Sir James Douglas, nicknamed 'The Good' and the father of Archibald, but a similar uprising took place after the usurpation of the Scottish crown by Edward Balliol in 1332. It was not until 1353 that William Douglas, cousin to Archibald, finally destroyed the Balliol's stranglehold on Galloway. It was no doubt in recognition of these services that David II honoured the house of Douglas with an earldom, first conferred on William in 1357, as well as bestowing on Archibald the wardenship of the Scottish West March. The acquisition of the lordship of Galloway, together with the purchase of the earldom of Wigtown in 1372 from the troubled Thomas Fleming, greatly increased the Douglas family's landed possessions, although, for the most part, the area was inhabited by a people not favourably disposed towards them. The building of a strong castle was a necessity and the island of Threave was selected by Archibald as the site for his baronial seat.

A silver penny of Edward I of England, minted in London c 1300. Found amongst building debris to the south of the tower house, it is one of few proofs that the island was a stronghold before the arrival of the Black Douglas.

There is scant information from the written record concerning the castle during the Douglas period. Archibald, as lord of Galloway and heir to the earldom of Douglas (which he received in 1388), could not have resided for any length of time there. His attendance at the royal court and Parliament necessitated his lodging for much of his life elsewhere and, as earl, his attendance at the various other baronial seats, such as Douglas and Abercorn, was imperative. In addition, his marriage to Joanna Moray (c 1362) added Bothwell Castle and extensive estates in the north of Scotland to his charge. The castle would appear to have been a more permanent place of residence for Princess Margaret Stewart, eldest daughter of Robert III and wife of Archibald, fourth earl of Douglas, son of 'The Grim'. Following her husband's untimely death at the battle of Verneuil in 1424, Margaret continued to reside at the castle from where were issued several charters relating to grants of land within the lordship of Galloway—over which she ruled after her husband's demise. She probably died at the castle and was buried in the chancel of Lincluden Church, Dumfries.

Her grand-daughter Margaret, better known as 'The Fair Maid of Galloway', inherited the lordship and her marriage in 1444 to her second cousin, William, eighth earl of Douglas, in an attempt to consolidate the vast Douglas estates, led to a final confrontation with the new king, James II. He was determined to put an end to the autocratic powers of the major aristocratic families, of whom the Black Douglases were supreme. Firstly in 1450, the earldom of Wigtown was annexed to the crown and this was followed in 1452 by the assassination of the eighth earl by the young king himself when dining together at Stirling Castle. The ninth earl's resolve to avenge his brother's death led to a third and final attempt by the king, in 1455, to destroy the Black Douglas. A systematic destruction of all the major Douglas strongholds was undertaken until by the beginning of June only the island fortress of Threave was holding out. Items of crown

A portrait of James II (1437-60) by an unknown artist. His vendetta against the Black Douglas brought him in person to Threave to supervise the siege. Taking up temporary residence at Tongland Abbey, near Kirkcudbright, he watched his cherished cannon bombard the castle. Five years later, at the siege of Roxburgh he was to perish from injuries sustained when a nearby '. . . misformed gun . . . brake in shooting'. (Reproduced by kind permission of the National Galleries of Scotland)

expenditure for this period provide the only accurate historical record of the nature of the siege. It was to last for more than two months and necessitated the presence of the king in person who took up temporary residence in nearby Tongland Abbey. A small tent for his personal use at the siege was made by Duncan Taylor from materials provided by certain Edinburgh merchants and, when it became apparent that the besieged were prepared for a lengthy stay, the king ordered William, earl of Orkney and chancellor of Scotland, to arrange for and accompany the transportation of a 'great bombard' (the name for the giant siege guns of the time; it was certainly not Mons Meg which was not then in the country), from the arsenal within Linlithgow Palace to the island. With him travelled John Were, burgess of Linlithgow,

nd a friar, Andrew Lisouris, the king's
rpenter. The journey was not without
cident for the weighty piece of ordnance
oke a wheel of its gun-carriage and sank
to the bog over Crawfordmuir causing the
own to expend £12 6s 0d on its extrication.
he garrison ultimately surrendered but the
cord of payments from the exchequer to
hn Fraser, custodian, John Dunbar and
thers in the castle during the siege perhaps
dicates that the place capitulated, not
rough fear of the ordnance, but by
ersuasion of a more subtle nature.

The castle from the north end of the island. The artillery fortification could well have been the product of the inventive mind of John Dunbar, a squire of the Black Douglas who resided at Duchrae, a few miles to the north, but who was amongst the garrison during the 1455 siege. Shortly thereafter he became, for a while, master gunsmith to James II and was with the king at his death at Roxburgh five years later. He was a frequent visitor to the Low Countries, at that time the centre of the ordnance industry.

n attack on a castle, from a German Firework Book, *ntemporary with the 1455 siege. A large wrought-iron siege gun great bombard') in the foreground is trained on the castle while ot-soldiers contribute to the onslaught by firing incendiary rows. The garrison within, largely concentrated at the wall-ad, returns fire using cross-bows and smaller guns.*

The castle under crown control

The whole of the lordship of Galloway was immediately annexed to the crown and the castle placed under the custody of, firstly, Sir Alexander Boyd of Drumcoll, then William Edmondstone, the king's cousin, under whose control the castle was furnished with guns and £40 13s 6d spent on repairs to the arsenal ('domus artilarie').

Revenue for the upkeep of the castle and the wages bill of the garrison was met from the surrounding farmlands (granges) of Kelton and Threave itself. In addition, the custodian of the castle had all rights to the fishing in the river as well as control over the mill at Kelton. The king himself does not appear to have stayed at the castle for any length of time, his recorded visit in 1460 being *en route* to Roxburgh.

William Edmondstone's successors as keeper, Humphrey Colquhoun and David Crichton, lasted only a short while before the castle was granted in jointure to Margaret of Denmark by her husband James III in 1473. Robert, Lord Carlisle became the new keeper, a post he combined with the stewardship of Kirkcudbright. Others followed, including Archibald, fifth earl of Angus, Patrick, earl of Bothwell and James Dunbar of Blackcrag, before custody of the castle was eventually declared heritable in the family of Lord Maxwell in 1526.

A greater insight into the everyday life of the castle survives from the early years of royal occupation. The transportation of pieces of ordnance and other artillery from Threave to Edinburgh is frequently referred to. A local carpenter, John McLellan, was paid £5 6s 8d in 1460 for repairs to the roof and other odd jobs and the provisioning of the island in case of siege cost the royal exchequer £10 in 1489. The most interesting information to survive concerns the visit of James IV in 1502. For his increased comfort a large quantity of woollen cloth and other material, all brightly coloured, was sent by horse to the castle to improve the existing furnishings. One of the king's falconers, Alexander Law, was also requested to make his way to Threave. The then keeper and host, Sir John Dunbar of Mochrum, expended £14 on a cask of red wine, a cask of claret, and a quantity of wheat, and two head of cattle for the royal guest. The consumption of all this fare probably accounts for one strange item in the accounts of the Lord High Treasurer, that of a payment by the king to the 'ald lutair' (old luteplayer) who resided in the castle.

The castle continued to play a role in the turbulent history of Anglo-Scottish relations until the Union of the Crowns. A letter from the English Privy Council to the earl of Hertford in April, 1544 stated Henry VIII's desire to have Threave in his charge and the capture of the then keeper, Robert, Lord Maxwell at the Battle of Solway Moss in 1542 made this all the more easy. After a brief spell in English hands Threave was eventually restored to Scotland in 1545 after a short siege. The Maxwell family were, however, allowed to remain keepers though they were frequently suspected of treachery. Both Mary Queen of Scots and James VI (in 1565 and 1568 repectively) demanded the rendering of the castle, its garrison and the artillery into their hands. In the uncertain days before the arrival of the Spanish Armada, the Roman Catholic John, Lord Maxwell, was suspected of treason and the castle was ordered to be surrendered. It was not readily done and so pressure was brought to bear on him by an otherwise unwarlike James VI.

Following the Union of the Crowns the castle's role as an important fortress on the Anglo-Scottish Border declined. In 1606 John Lord Maxwell was arrested by the crown, not for treason as his forbears had been, but for the trifling crime of not paying his taxes on Threave Castle and elsewhere. The keepership was temporarily held by the Ker family before reverting yet again to Lord Maxwell. By 1638, Robert Maxwell, earl of Nithsdale had become a steady supporter of Charles I in that monarch's dispute with the Scottish Committee of Estates, an alliance that was to lead to the final overthrow of the island fortress. As conflict approached, the earl garrisoned the castle with 70 men and enough arms, ammunition and provisions to withstand a lengthy siege. In 1640 that number was increased to 100 after the keeper had been ordered to surrender to the Committee of Estates under pain of treason. The order was disregarded and the Covenanters, under the leadership of Lieutenant Colonel John Hume, laid siege to the castle. Heavy pieces of ordnance were used, though apparently with little effect. The garrison held out for 13 weeks until, in September of that year, a letter from Charles himself to the earl authorised surrender, enabling the garrison to walk free with honour. An initial decision to garrison the castle was soon overturned by the War Committee and an order was issued authorising the laird of Balmaghie to dismantle the house so that it could not be

The castle in 1789 as drawn by Captain Grose. The gaping hole in the artillery fortification to the right of the gatehouse was caused by the Covenanters' artillery in 1640. Two of the three circular towers have since collapsed into the ditch. The entrance into the tower house has yet to be altered in preparation for the receipt of prisoners taken in the French wars.

used again. The laird's instructions were:

'. . . that the sklait roofe of the hous and battlement thairof to be taken downe with the lofting thairof, dores and windowes of the samen, and to stop the vault of the said hows; and with power to the said Lard of Balmaghie to use and dispose upon the tymber, stanes, iron worke, to the use of the publict; his necessar charges and expenses being deducted. And ordaines him, during the slighting thairof, to put sex musqueteires and ane sergand thairin, to be enterteanit upon the publict.'

The island fortress was never again inhabited, though minor works were carried out at the beginning of the nineteenth century to make it suitable as a prison for captives from the French wars. In 1913 the owner, Edward Gordon, entrusted the property to HM Office of Works. The lands belonging to the Gordon family have subsequently been bequeathed to the National Trust for Scotland though the castle itself still remains in state care.

The castle from across the eastern channel of the River Dee. During its occupation, the castle and island were reached either by boat crossing the western channel or on foot or horseback via the ford at the southern end of the island (off to the left in the photograph).

'This Tall Forbidding Tower'

The tower house

For us to picture the castle as it would have appeared in Archibald Douglas' day we must forget, for the moment, the low masonry artillery fortification and ditch that now surrounds the tower house. This tall, forbidding tower originally stood alone, a self-contained domestic unit fully capable of being defended by the men-at-arms temporarily stationed within its massive walls. Its defence was largely conducted from the wall-head 26 m above the ground. Here, resting on the flat roof, large machines would assail the besiegers with assorted projectiles whilst those who had penetrated to the bases of the walls would be open to attack from the besieged standing in a covered gallery projecting from the wall-top. A triple row of put-log holes into which this gallery was fitted is visible around three of the four sides.

The tower house was designed to accommodate the family of the Black Douglas alone. The many men-at-arms, household and domestic staff lived elsewhere in the neighbourhood, some on the island itself. Traces of these less substantial structures have been found grouped around the east and south sides of the tower, together with stores, workshops and outbuildings. The islanders carried out wood-turning, cord-waining, smithing and leadsmelting and the plentiful food debris highlights a good standard of animal husbandry.

Stone foundations of two large, two-storeyed(?) structures were found during excavation to the south-east of the tower house. Both built contemporaneously with the tower house to provide accommodation for men-at-arms, retainers and guests of the Black Douglas. The hasty measures taken to strengthen the island's defences c 1450 resulted in their being dismantled, not only to provide a handy source of stone for the new artillery fortification but also to give the gunners within an unimpeded view of the higher ground to the east and whence James II's expected assault would come.

Cross the ditch via the drawbridge.
The tower house had only one entrance. As we see it today it is the product of the early nineteenth century when work was carried out to prepare the castle for prisoners from the Napoleonic wars. Originally the threshold was a little higher and the doorway wider, culminating in what is now the semi-circular window. The door was reached by a moveable timber stair which could be removed inside the tower in time of siege. Those intent on battering down the door were exposed to attack from defenders in the projecting gallery directly above. Unlike the gallery around the other three sides, which was a temporary feature, that over the door was permanent and two of the projecting corbel-stones that formed it have survived the 1640 dismantling.

Enter the tower house.
The doorway gives access into the second the tower's five storeys. This was formerly divided into two chambers by a timber partition, that on the left serving as a kitch that on the right as a reception hall with access in the far corner to a spiral stair lead

A cut-away reconstruction drawing of the tower house, by Geoffrey Hay. Note in particular the defensive arrangements at roof level.

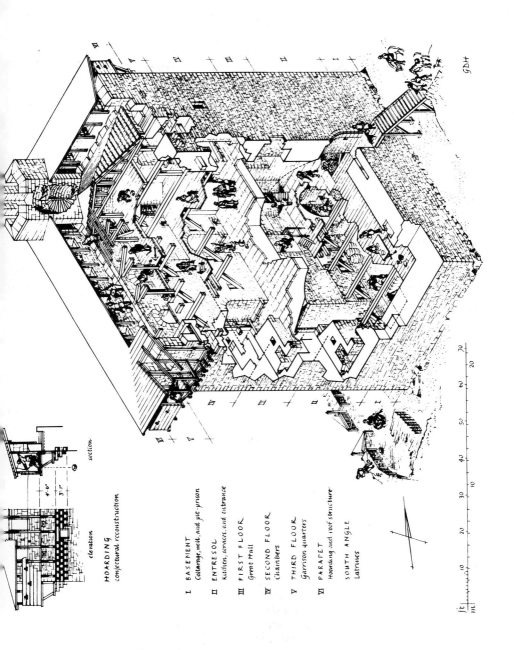

The hall and upper chambers, looking south. The Black Douglas, aware of the hostility of the native Gallovidians, restricted the provision of windows to the relatively sunless, though considerably safer, north and west walls facing onto the river. Nonetheless, they too have been made more secure by the addition of iron grilles and massive wooden shutters.

to the upper storeys. The basement served as cellarage, including a well, and was reached from the kitchen by a ladder and hatch. A dark, dank **prison** occupied the basement beneath the reception hall. One Adam Crossar, a petty thief, was confined here in 1579.

Ascend the stair.
Here on the third storey was the principal apartment—the **hall**. Originally it would have presented an imposing spectacle with its plastered walls draped in coloured hangings and the oak ceiling brightly painted. The warm glow from the fireplace and the shafts of light penetrating the translucent glass-paned windows would have completed a picture which was destroyed with the coming of the Covenanters in 1640. The laird of Balmaghie's dismantling programme resulted in the removal of all timber and ironwork as well as much of the dressed freestone, particularly that forming the fireplace. Consolidation work by HM Office of Works the early 1900s is immediately recognisable the unpointed random masonry infill set a little from the face of the wall.

Above the hall were two **bed-chambers** served by a latrine closet in the south-west corner. The more southerly of the two fireplaces has an unusual flat 'joggled' lin the stones of which were found in the basement and set back into place by HM Office of Works.

The chamber above is most unusual. Th is neither fireplace nor latrine, simply nin windows and, curiously, a door in the sou east corner. Such a chamber can only have served as temporary quarters for the men-arms during a siege, the windows affordir excellent all-round panoramas and the do perhaps housing a winch for hoisting war machines and projectiles to this storey and the roof and wall-walk immediately above

Leave the tower house and view the artillery fortification.

A fireplace in the more southerly of the two bed-chambers abo the hall.

The rear of the artillery fortification. The wall-walk, gatehouse and circular towers were reached by timber staging and ladders placed against the stonework. All that survive today are the odd joist-hole (far right in the photograph) and roof-raggle (see the south face of the tower house).

The artillery fortification

The low masonry wall around the tower house is the artillery fortification ('domus artilarie') built by William, the eighth earl, about 1450. The walls themselves have simple vertical slits through which defenders with conventional long-bows and cross-bows could fire. The three circular towers, however, were designed to accommodate small guns, the development of which was then very much in

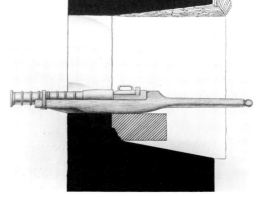

Conjectural reconstruction of the gun used in the circular towers of the artillery fortification at the time of the 1455 siege. Made of built-up flat wrought-iron bars bound with iron hoops passed over and shrunk on, this breech-loading cannon, firing gunstones up to three inches in diameter, was mounted on a wooden stock attached to a sill-beam set into the recess visible on either side of the gunloop.

15

Among the countless objects found in the harbour were a platter and bowl made from ash, the former with a 'heart' (the principal heraldic device of the Black Douglas) branded into the under-side. In the foreground is an oak paddle blade.

its infancy. Two of these towers were badly damaged in the 1640 siege and have subsequently collapsed. The third at the south-east corner is complete, though minus its two timber floors, and gives us an idea of the field of vision available to the gunner.

The fortification to the west of the tower along the river-bank, now reduced to its foundations, was never as substantial as the rest. Here is enclosed a rock-cut harbour into which was brought the bulk of the provisions for the islanders, ferried across the river in small boats from the opposite bank. During excavation of the water-logged silts within the harbour parts from these boats were found together with a host of assorted artefacts ranging from leather shoes and sword-scabbards to iron keys, cross-bow bolts and an almost complete wooden barrel containing gun-stones.

Further Reading

W Fraser, *The Douglas Book* (Edinburgh 1885)
D MacGibbon and T Ross, *The Castellated and Domestic Architecture of Scotland*, vol 1 (Edinburgh 1887).
Royal Commission on the Ancient and Historical Monuments of Scotland, *Stewartry of Kirkcudbright* (Edinburgh 1914).
R Nicholson, *Scotland: The Later Middle Ages* (Edinburgh 1974).
G L Good and C J Tabraham, 'Excavations at Threave Castle, Galloway, 1974-78', *Medieval Archaeology,* vol 25 (1981), 90-140.
G L Good and C J Tabraham, 'The Artillery Fortification at Threave Castle, Galloway', in D H Caldwell (ed), *Scottish Weapons and Fortifications* (Edinburgh 1981).
S Cruden, *The Scottish Castle* (Edinburgh 1981).
C J Tabraham, *Scottish Castles and Fortifications* (Edinburgh 1986).